FUN WITH SCIENCE

SOUND

TERRY CASH

Contents

Use the symbols below to help you
identify the three kinds of practical
activities in this book.

EXPERIMENTS

TRICKS

THINGS TO MAKE

Illustrated by Kuo Kang Chen · Peter Bull

KING*f*ISHER

Introduction

Sit still, close your eyes and listen. Sounds are all around you. Even on the quietest night there are sounds such as distant traffic, rustling leaves or the sound of your own heart beating. Which of the sounds are natural sounds, made by animals, trees, people or the wind? Which of the sounds are made by machines working? Are the sounds loud, noisy, quiet or musical?

The experiments in the first part of this book will help you to discover how sounds are made and how our ears help us to hear sounds. In the second half of the book, you can investigate how musical instruments produce sounds and find out how to make a variety of simple instruments, such as drums, an elastic band guitar, a glass xylophone, tubular bells, a packing case bass and a one-string banjo.

The questions on these two pages are based on the scientific ideas explained in this book. As you carry out the experiments, you will be able to answer these questions and understand more about sounds in the world around you.

This book covers six main topics:
- What is sound?
- Hearing sounds, echoes, acoustics, noise
- The speed of sound
- Music from strings or pipes; pitch
- Percussion instruments; recorded music
- Animal sounds

A blue line (like the one around the edge of these two pages) indicates the start of a new topic.

▲ Why do sound waves from a tuning fork make the water splash? (page 7)

▼ Why do we hear a sonic boom when Concorde flies overhead? (page 19)

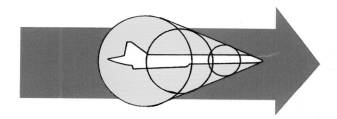

▼ How are echoes used to detect shoals of fish? (page 15)

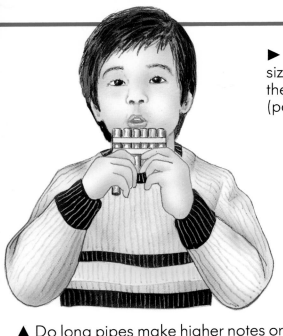

▶ How does the size of a drum affect the sound it makes? (page 33)

▲ Do long pipes make higher notes or lower notes than short pipes? (page 29)

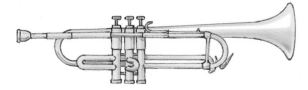

▲ Why does a trumpet player need to 'blow raspberries'? (page 28)

▼ How do our ears filter out unwanted noises? (page 16)

▲ How can you vary the pitch of the notes made by twanging a ruler? (page 22)

▼ On this elastic band guitar, do the tightly stretched bands make high notes or low notes? (page 27)

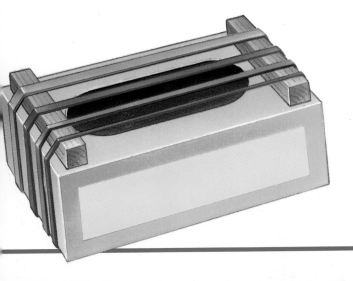

▶ Why does the sound made by the siren of a moving vehicle drop to a lower note as the vehicle passes you? (page 18)

Making Sounds

From singing and stamping to clapping and clicking your fingers, you can make all sorts of sounds with different parts of your body. Try copying the sounds of animals or objects such as a clock or a car. How many different sounds can you make?

▶ Ventriloquists can use their own voices to make a model of a person or an animal look as if it is speaking. To do this, ventriloquists have to learn how to speak without moving their lips. You can try this yourself, but it takes a lot of practice.

Whistle, Hoot or Pop

Whistle
Loud whistles are made with your fingers and lips. Curl your tongue back slightly and place the first and second fingers of each hand into your mouth so that the tips of your second fingers just touch together underneath your tongue.

Now blow through the small gap between your lips and your fingers. You will feel the air rushing out between your lips and, with practice, you should produce a whistling sound.

Hoot
To hoot like an owl, cup your hands together with your thumbs side by side. Make a little gap between your thumbs and blow gently across the hole – not straight into it. It will take some practice to get this right, but keep trying.

Snap and Click

Can you snap your fingers? First push your thumb and middle finger together. Keep pushing, but slide your thumb to one side so that your middle finger snaps down into your palm with a loud click. It helps if your fingers are slightly damp. With practice you should be able to snap two fingers at the same time.

More things to try

- When people are frightened, they say their knees 'knock'. Can you 'knock' your knees together to make a sound?
- Do your teeth 'chatter' when you are cold?
- Beat your chest like a drum. Then do the same thing while you shout "Aaahh!". How does the sound change?

Pop

Have you heard a cork being pulled from a bottle? If it is pulled out quickly, air suddenly rushes into the neck of the bottle and makes a loud, popping sound.

To make the same sound, put your first finger into your mouth and make a small, round 'O' shape with your lips. Press the pad of your fingertip against the inside of your cheek and flick it firmly out of your mouth.

▲ In the Spanish dance called flamenco the dancer clicks her fingers above her head in time with the music. Sometimes castanets are held in the hands and used to make the clicking sounds.

Shaking the Air

All things which make a sound have one thing in common – they make the air shake back and forth very fast. These shaking movements are called **vibrations**. If the vibrations reach our ears, we 'hear' the sound – *see pages 8–9*.

Sound Waves

A sound makes tiny particles (molecules) in the air bump into each other. When this happens, the molecules are first squashed together, and then expand again, so passing on their energy to the molecules next to them. Individual molecules vibrate slightly to and fro but do not move through the air. The vibrations passing from molecule to molecule are what we call **sound waves**.

You can see how this works by using a row of marbles to represent molecules in the air.

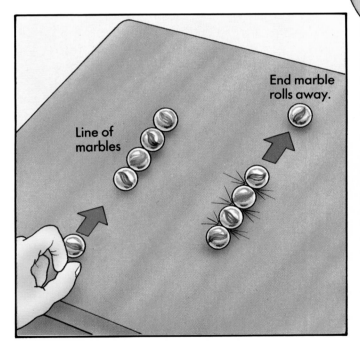

End marble rolls away.

Line of marbles

Arrange four marbles in a line. Then flick a fifth marble so it hits one end of the line. One by one, each marble will hit the next one and pass energy along the line. When the fourth marble receives the energy, it will roll away.

Seeing Vibrations

Put a few grains of rice on a drum skin and tap the skin gently. The vibrations of the drum skin, stretched tight over the frame, will make the rice dance and jump. If you tap the skin harder, what happens to the rice?

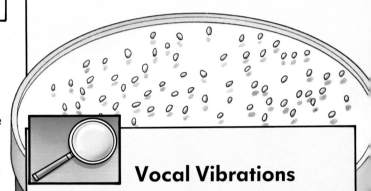

Vocal Vibrations

Hold your fingers against your throat while you speak. Can you feel the sound? When you speak, shout or sing, air is pushed from your lungs over flaps of muscle called **vocal cords**, which are at the top of your windpipe. The air rushing over your vocal cords makes them vibrate and this generates the sound of your voice. Women have higher voices than men because their vocal cords are shorter and more tightly stretched.

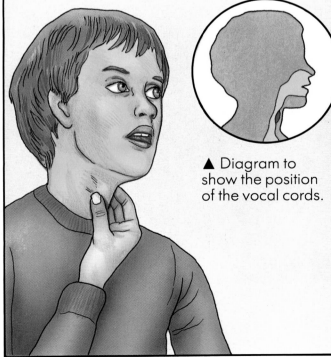

▲ Diagram to show the position of the vocal cords.

You can also see vibrations with a tuning fork and a glass of water.

Tap the tuning fork on the palm of your hand and hold the fork against the surface of some water in a glass. Can you see how the vibrations of the fork make the water shake?

Hint
After this investigation, dry the tuning fork thoroughly.

Make a Sound Cannon

This trick shows you how to blow out a candle with sound waves.

Equipment: A cardboard tube, some thin, clinging plastic wrap or pieces cut from a plastic bag, scissors, sticky tape, a small candle, a saucer or dish, sand or soil.

1. Cover both ends of the tube with clinging plastic wrap or tape a piece of plastic tightly across each end.
2. Use the scissors to make a small hole in the plastic at one end of the tube.
3. Put some sand or soil in the saucer or dish and stand a small birthday-cake candle in the sand or soil.
4. Ask an adult to light the candle for you.
5. Hold the end of your 'sound cannon' with

the hole in it about 2–3 cm (1 inch) away from the candle flame.
6. When you tap the other end of the tube with your finger, the flame should go out.

How it works
It will sound as if you have tapped a small drum. The vibrations from the plastic drum skin will push the air inside the tube out through the small hole in the plastic with enough force to blow out the candle.

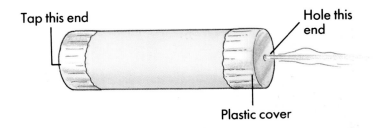

Tap this end

Hole this end

Plastic cover

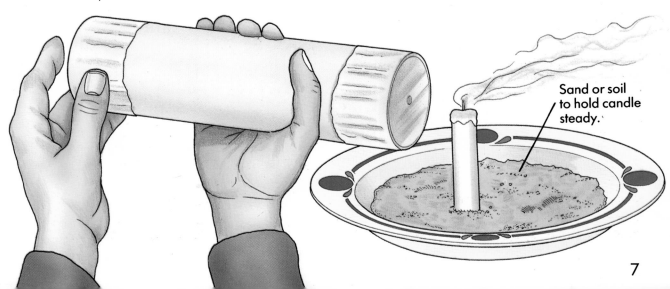

Sand or soil to hold candle steady.

Hearing Sounds

The next six pages will help you to understand how our ears enable us to hear the sounds around us.

Looking at the Ear

The ear is an amazing and complex part of the body. The bit that sticks out of the side of your head, the outer ear, is only part of the ear. The rest of the ear is inside your head.

The outer ear
The outer ear is shaped like a funnel to collect sounds and direct them inside your head. The sounds, in the form of vibrating air, hit a thin sheet of skin called the **eardrum** and make it shake.

The middle ear
Here, three tiny bones, the **hammer** (malleus), the **anvil** (incus), and the **stirrup** (stapes), increase (amplify) the vibrations from the eardrum and pass them on to the inner ear.

The inner ear
In the inner ear, a shell-shaped organ called the **cochlea** changes the vibrations into electrical messages. These messages are carried to the brain along nerves. The brain interprets the messages it receives and we 'hear' the sounds.

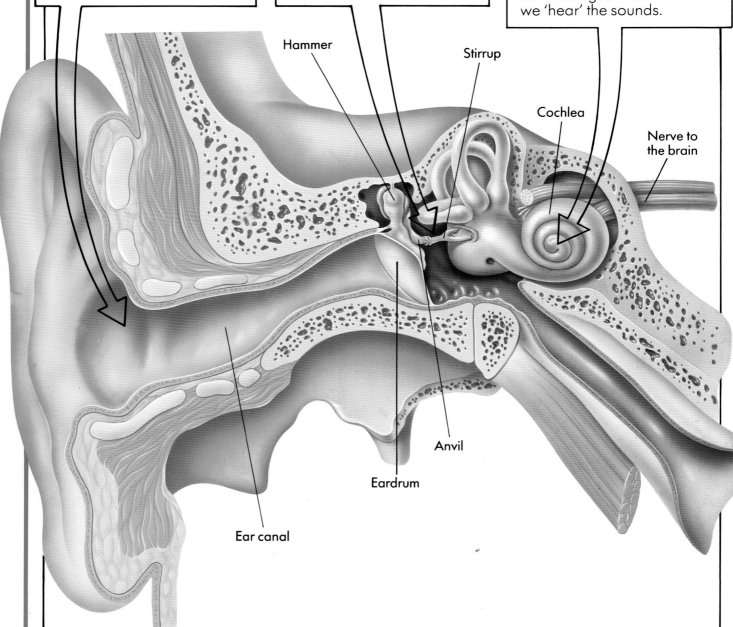

Hammer

Stirrup

Cochlea

Nerve to the brain

Anvil

Eardrum

Ear canal

How Good is Your Hearing?

Equipment: A tiny object, such as a pin, a ruler, notebook and pencil.

Ask a friend to help you with this experiment.
1. Ask your friend to stand with his back to the table.
2. Drop the pin on to the table from a height of about 10 cm (4 inches). Make sure you drop the pin from the same height each time – check the height with the ruler.
3. Ask your friend to put up his hand if he can hear the pin hitting the table.
4. Measure the distance from the table to your friend and make a note of the distance.
5. Then ask your friend to take two steps further away and repeat the experiment until he can no longer hear the pin drop.
6. Try the same experiment on some other friends and compare your results.

Drop pin from same height each time.

Where is the Sound Coming From?

We can usually tell where a sound is coming from. To tell the direction of a sound, we turn the head until the sound can be heard equally strongly with both ears.

Many other animals, such as horses and rabbits, can swivel their long ears in many directions. This helps them to sense danger, such as the approach of an enemy.

Ask some friends to help you test how good our ears are at telling the direction of a sound.

Blindfold a volunteer and stand in a ring around him or her. Take turns to make a gentle noise, such as a clap of hands, a click of the fingers or a quiet call. After each sound, the person with the blindfold should point to where they think the sound is coming from. How good are they at pin-pointing the direction?

Then try the same experiment with an ear muff or a pad of cotton wool over one of the person's ears. Does this make their sense of direction better or worse?

Blindfold

Making Sounds Louder

Most of us are able to hear well. But as we grow older, our hearing usually becomes less sensitive, and some people may also experience temporary or permanent deafness as a result of disease.

Some people with hearing problems can be helped by wearing a hearing aid. This is a miniature electrical amplifier which is fitted behind or inside the ear. It makes sounds much louder and passes them straight into the ear canal.

▶ A megaphone is used when a person is speaking to a large crowd of people, in order to increase the sound of their voice.

Make an Ear Trumpet

Roll a large sheet of paper or card into a cone shape and tape the ends to hold them in place. The cone should be as wide as possible at one end and narrow enough at the other end to fit comfortably into your ear.

When you put the ear trumpet to your ear, notice how much louder sounds appear to be. If you point the trumpet towards a quiet sound on the other side of a room, you should be able to hear the sound clearly.

By turning the trumpet around and shouting into the narrow end, you can make your voice sound louder.

How it works
The trumpet collects sounds and directs them into your ear canal, so you can hear more easily. When you shout into the trumpet, it concentrates the sound energy and stops it from being lost so quickly. This is why your voice sounds louder.

Tick-tock Trick

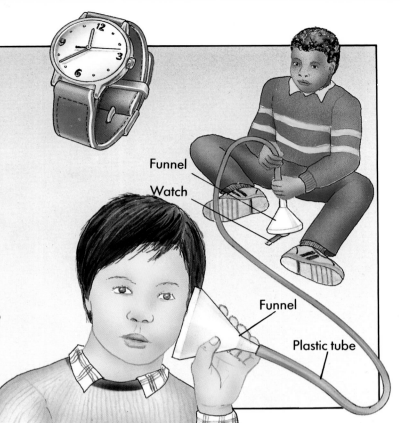

Funnel

Watch

Funnel

Plastic tube

Equipment: Two plastic funnels, about 2 metres (6 feet) of plastic tubing, a mechanical watch or clock (not a digital one).

1. Push one funnel into either end of the tubing.
2. Place the watch on the floor about 2 metres (6 feet) away.
3. Ask a friend to hold one of the funnels over the watch and put the other funnel to your ear. You should be able to hear the watch ticking quite clearly.
4. Experiment with other quiet sounds.

Make a Tube Telephone

You can use the funnels and plastic tubing to make a telephone. It is more fun if you have a long piece of tubing; tape several pieces of tubing together if necessary.

Warning
Don't shout. You could damage your hearing.

Give one end of the telephone to a friend and take the other end into another room. Take it in turns to whisper messages to one another.

11

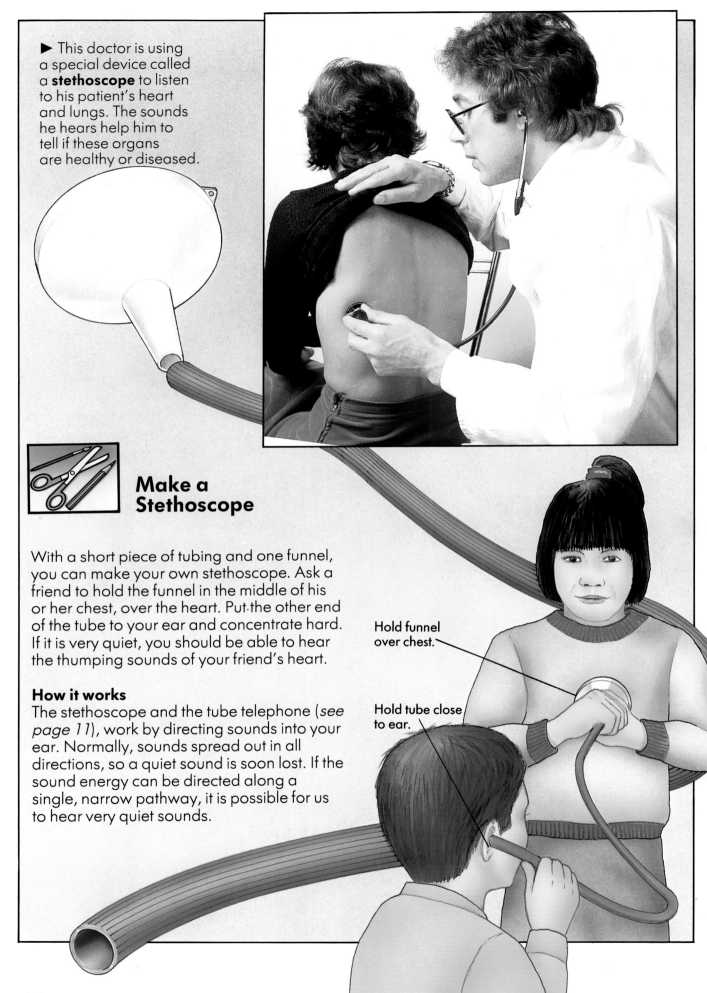

► This doctor is using a special device called a **stethoscope** to listen to his patient's heart and lungs. The sounds he hears help him to tell if these organs are healthy or diseased.

Make a Stethoscope

With a short piece of tubing and one funnel, you can make your own stethoscope. Ask a friend to hold the funnel in the middle of his or her chest, over the heart. Put the other end of the tube to your ear and concentrate hard. If it is very quiet, you should be able to hear the thumping sounds of your friend's heart.

How it works
The stethoscope and the tube telephone (*see page 11*), work by directing sounds into your ear. Normally, sounds spread out in all directions, so a quiet sound is soon lost. If the sound energy can be directed along a single, narrow pathway, it is possible for us to hear very quiet sounds.

Hold funnel over chest.

Hold tube close to ear.

Make a Yogurt Pot Telephone

A yogurt pot telephone works in a different way from a tube telephone, but it still uses the vibrations from your voice.

Equipment: Two yogurt pots, string, scissors.

1. Use the scissors to make a hole in the bottom of each pot.
2. Push one end of the string through the hole in one pot and the other end through the hole in the other pot. Knot the string to stop it pulling out of the holes.
3. To use your telephone, stand facing a friend and pull the string tight.
4. Hold your pot to your ear while your friend talks slowly and clearly into the other pot.

— Keep the string tight.

Knot in string

How it works

The vibrations of your friend's voice make their pot shake. The pot makes the string shake and the string passes the vibrations on to your pot. You hear the vibrations as your friend's voice. Why does a yogurt pot telephone work only if the string is held straight and tight?

Sound Reflections

When sound waves hit a barrier, such as a cliff, they bounce back and we hear the sound again. This reflected sound is called **echo**. Out in an open space, an echo is fainter because the vibrations spread out in all directions and lose energy. But in an enclosed space, such as a tunnel, the reflected sound cannot escape and the echoes are very loud.

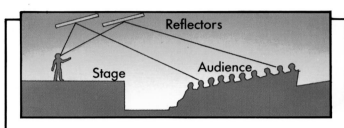

Echoes and Acoustics

Acoustics is the study of how the quality of sound is affected by the shape of a room and the materials it is made from. Acoustics is important in concert halls and theatres where sounds need to be clearly heard.

If there are too many echoes bouncing to and fro between the walls, the audience will hear a confusing jumble of noises. This is called **reverberation**. To reduce the amount of reverberation, a concert hall can be specially shaped and made from materials which absorb sound well, such as wood.

Experiment with Echoes

A good place to find out more about echoes is near a solid wall of rock, such as a cliff. If you face the cliff and shout loudly, the sound of your voice will travel to the cliff and be reflected back at you. If the sound is reflected from different parts of the cliff, you may hear several echoes, as if there were lots of people answering you.

Echoes under the Sea

Echoes can be used to detect shoals of fish, submarines or wrecked ships on the sea bed. Sound waves are sent down into the sea from an instrument called an echo-sounder on board a ship. The time taken for the echoes to bounce back to the ship can be used to work out the position and shape of any objects beneath the ship. It can also be used to map the depth and contours of the sea bed.

This technique is called SONAR – **So**und **N**avigation **a**nd **R**anging. SONAR is so sensitive it can show the difference between one large fish and a shoal of little ones.

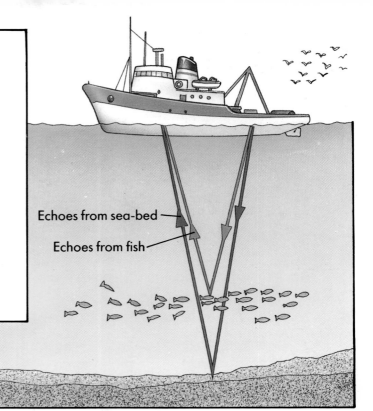

Echoes from sea-bed

Echoes from fish

Animal Echoes

Bats make high squeaking sounds and use their sensitive ears to pick up the echoes from objects around them. The echoes give the bats information about the position and size of objects and help them to work out if objects are moving. This technique is called **echo-location**. It helps bats to find their way in the dark and capture food, such as flying insects.

We cannot hear the echo-squeaks made by bats but we can hear some of the other sounds they make.

Echoes bouncing off insect.

High squeaks sent out by bat.

▶ A long-eared bat using echo-location to catch a moth for its supper.

Too Much Noise

Sounds which we find unpleasant, we often call **noise**. Noise is made by an irregular pattern of sound waves. Too much noise can damage our hearing and affect body processes such as digestion. It is illegal to make noise above a certain level and some measures (such as fitting cars with silencers) can reduce or prevent noise. But noise pollution is still a serious problem, especially in big cities where vast numbers of people and machines are crowded together.

Measuring Noise

The loudness of a sound can be found by measuring the energy of a sound wave. Loudness is usually measured in **decibels**. A sound of zero decibels is just too faint for the human ear to hear. An ordinary conversation can produce more than 50 decibels of sound energy. In a street full of heavy traffic, the noise is likely to be about 80 decibels or more.

Rustling leaves	10
Whisper	20
Ordinary conversation	40–60
Vacuum cleaner	70
Heavy traffic	90
Pneumatic drill	100
Aircraft engine	100–200
Space rocket	200+

▲People who use very noisy machines protect their hearing by wearing special ear defenders.

Filtering out Noises

When we are trying to concentrate on a particular task in a noisy place, our hearing system can filter out unwanted sounds.

To see how this works, turn on a tape recorder and read a passage from your favourite book to a friend. After about a minute, stop the tape recorder and ask your friend to tell you what they have just heard. They will remember your reading, but what about any other sounds?

Now turn up the volume and play back the tape. You will be surprised at how many different sounds you can hear in the background. A tape recorder cannot select the sounds it wants to hear in the way we can.

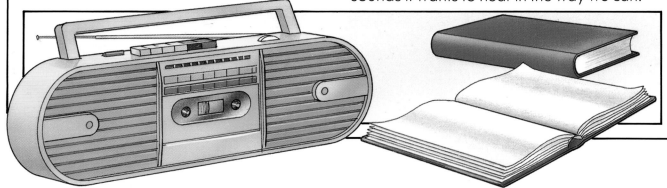

Exploding Bag Trick

Scrunch up the neck of a paper bag and blow into the bag so it puffs up. Hold the neck of the bag tightly and clap the palm of your other hand hard against it. The bag will burst with a loud bang.

The air trapped inside the bag is squashed by your hand and splits through the paper with a lot of force. You hear this as an explosion of sound.

BANG

▲ If there are noises near a large accumulation of snow, the vibrations can cause an avalanche. Avalanches are sometimes started deliberately near ski resorts to prevent a dangerous build-up of snow.

Make a Paper Pistol

All you need is a double page from a tabloid newspaper or some brown wrapping paper about 30 cm by 40 cm (12 in by 16 in).

1. Fold the paper in half along the longest side and open it out again.
2. Fold each corner down to meet the line of the centre fold.
3. Fold the paper in half along the centre fold.
4. Fold the paper in half again, press down the crease firmly and open it out again.
5. Fold the widest corners down as shown in the diagram.
6. Fold the paper back to make a triangle shape.
7. To fire your paper pistol, hold it by the long ends and swish it sharply down through the air.

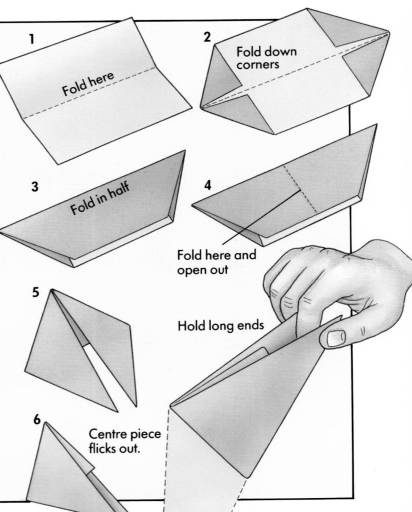

1 Fold here

2 Fold down corners

3 Fold in half

4 Fold here and open out

Hold long ends

5

6 Centre piece flicks out.

The Speed of Sound

A sound does not reach you the instant it is made; it takes time to travel to your ears. This can be difficult to understand unless you actually experience it. For example, if you attend an athletics meeting and sit some distance from the person with the starting gun, you will see the puff of smoke from the gun before you hear the bang. This is because light travels very fast indeed – at about 300,000 kilometres (186,416 miles) in one **second** – while sound travels much more slowly – at a speed of about 330 metres in one second (750 miles in an hour). So you will see the smoke instantly but the sound of the gun will not reach you until later.

Discovering the Speed of Sound

Early experiments to discover the speed of sound were carried out with a gun. A helper with a gun stood a measured distance from an observer with a stopwatch. On a given signal, the helper fired the gun into the air. As soon as the observer saw the flash of flame and smoke from the gun, she started the stopwatch. When she heard the bang from the gun, she stopped the watch. The time between seeing the flash and hearing the bang was the time taken for the sound to travel the measured distance.

The Doppler Effect

Have you ever noticed that the siren of a moving vehicle seems to drop to a lower note as it passes you? This is due to something called the **Doppler Effect**, which is named after Dr Christian Johann Doppler, who discovered the reason for it in 1842.

Dr Doppler found that if a source of sound is moving, the sound waves are squashed up ahead of it and stretched out behind it. If more sound waves per second reach your ears, you hear higher notes; if fewer sound waves per second reach your ears, you hear lower notes. As a vehicle with its siren blaring passes you, you hear the change from a high to a low note.

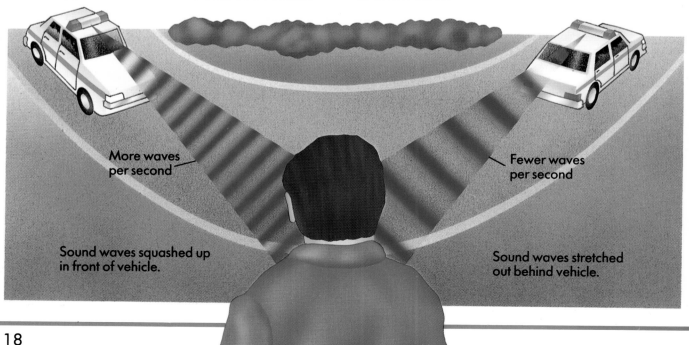

More waves per second

Fewer waves per second

Sound waves squashed up in front of vehicle.

Sound waves stretched out behind vehicle.

Measuring the Speed of Sound

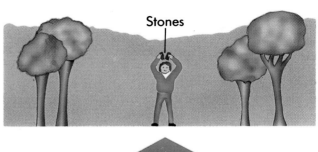

Stones

To measure the speed of sound, you will need a stopwatch and a long tape measure. Measure a distance of 500 metres (1640 feet) as accurately as possible. Ask a friend to stand at one end holding a large stone in each hand while you stand at the other end with the stopwatch. When you shout "Go," your friend should swing his hands together above his head, banging the stones as loudly as possible.

500-metre (1640-feet) distance

As soon as you see the stones clash together, start the watch and as soon as you hear the crack of them hitting each other, stop the watch. Record the time to the nearest tenth of a second. It is a good idea to repeat the experiment a number of times and take an average time.

To work out the speed of sound, use a calculator to divide the distance between you by the time.

Faster than Sound

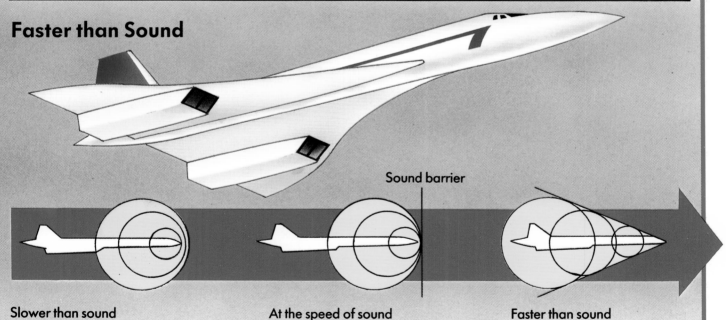

Sound barrier

Slower than sound   **At the speed of sound**   **Faster than sound**

A supersonic aircraft, such as Concorde, can fly faster than the speed of sound. As the aircraft approaches the speed of sound, it catches up with the sound waves travelling in front of it and pushes them against each other. This forms a barrier of squashed up (compressed) air in front of the aircraft. As the aircraft reaches the speed of sound, it overtakes this high-pressure air which spreads out behind the aircraft in a powerful 'shock wave'. People on the ground hear the shock wave as a noise like a loud clap of thunder. This is called the **sonic boom** and it has enough force to shatter windows.

Sound on the Move

Sound waves travel at different speeds through different materials. They travel faster through liquids (such as water) and solids (such as steel) than they do through air.

Hearing through Walls

If sounds are being made in a room, the vibrations in the air make the walls and doors vibrate too. Try holding an empty glass against the wall or door nearest to the sound. When you press your ear against the bottom of the glass, the sounds will be much clearer. The vibrating wall or door shakes the air inside the glass and the sounds are passed to your ear.

More things to try

Press your ear tightly against a wall while a friend taps the wall some distance away. You could make up a code and send secret messages to one another.

◀ Out in space, there is no air to carry sound vibrations. So when Dr Sally Ride speaks to other astronauts outside the air-pressurized cabin, or Mission Controllers on Earth, she has to use the radio. Radio waves are a type of electro-magnetic radiation and they can travel through space to the Earth.

Listening Underwater

As sound passes about five times faster through water than it does through air, sounds under the water will often seem much louder.

Lie on your back in the bath and keep your mouth and nose above the water but let your ears go under the surface. It will feel very strange at first but, if you listen carefully, your bath water will pass many sounds to you — including the sound of your own breathing. Tap the side of the bath gently and listen to the loud, booming sound that it makes.

Sounds in your Head

Tie some spoons in the middle of a length of string and jingle them together. You will hear a tinkling sound as the spoons knock against one another.

Now press the ends of the string hard against your ears and jingle the spoons again. How is the sound different?

Clench the handle of an ordinary dinner fork tightly between your teeth. Flick the ends of the prongs with your finger and you will hear strange, twanging sounds. Anyone watching you will hear only a faint flicking noise.

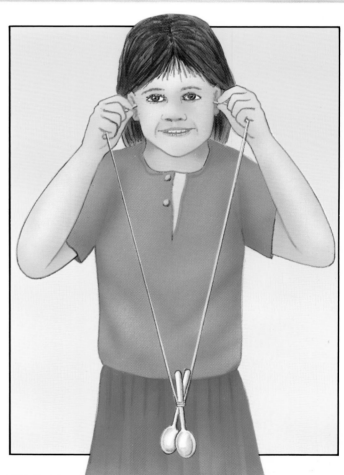

Warning
Do not flick the fork too hard. You might damage your teeth.

How it works
The vibrations from the spoons or the fork pass straight through the bones of your skull to reach your inner ear. The sounds are inside your head and you hear a much louder, deeper sound.

Musical Sounds

In the second half of this book, you can find out about musical sounds, which are made up of a series of notes. You can investigate how different instruments produce high and low notes and change the volume of the sounds they make. By making some simple musical instruments you can discover how string, brass and woodwind instruments produce their own distinctive musical sounds.

Playing the Ruler

Hold a rule on a table with half its length over the edge. Pluck the end of the ruler and listen to the sound.

Now move the ruler so there is only a short length over the edge of the table and pluck it again. Then try the same thing with a long length of ruler over the edge of the table.

As you move the ruler, what happens to the sound? If more of the ruler is over the edge of the table, does the sound become higher or lower?

Sound Boxes

Tap a tuning fork on the palm of your hand and touch the handle of the fork on to a table. What happens to the sound?

How it works
When the tuning fork touches the table, the sound becomes much louder. The vibrations of the fork make the table vibrate too. The table acts like a sound box, passing on its vibrations to the large area of air around it. The table **amplifies** (makes much louder) the sounds made by the fork.

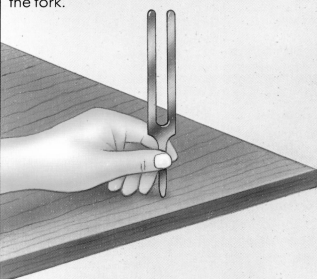

Most musical instruments have something to amplify the sounds they make. In a stringed instrument, such as an ordinary guitar or violin, the strings are stretched across a hollow box, which is usually made from wood. The vibrations of the strings make the wood and the air inside the box vibrate at the same rate as the strings. This is called **resonance**. It makes the sound louder and richer than it would be with the strings alone.

Make a Twanger

Equipment: A wire coat hanger, a pair of pliers or wire cutters, wire staples, a hammer, a block of wood about 15 cm by 10 cm (6 in by 4 in by 2 in).

1. Ask an adult to help you cut the coat hanger into five or six different lengths from 5 to 10 cm (2 to 4 inches) long.
2. Staple the lengths of wire on to the wood block with a hammer.
3. To play the twanger, pluck the wires with your thumbs.

How it works The vibrating wires would not make much sound by themselves but the wood block makes the sound much louder. Do longer lengths of wire make higher or lower notes?

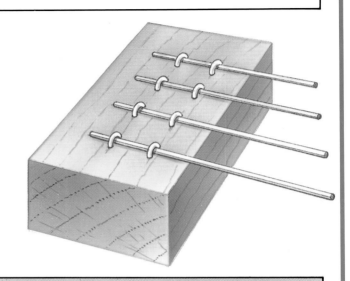

Make a Bull-roarer

You will need a piece of wood about the size of an ordinary ruler. Make a small hole in one end of the wood and tie a piece of string about 150 cm (5 feet) long through the hole.

To make your bull-roarer work, you will need a lot of space, so make sure there is no one standing too close to you. It is a good idea to try this experiment outdoors.

Hold the free end of the string and whirl the wood around your head. As the wood swings around, it makes the air vibrate with a strange roaring noise. Listen to the sound get louder as you swing the roarer faster and faster.

More things to try

Try using a larger, wider piece of wood. You will find that it makes a deeper, louder sound.

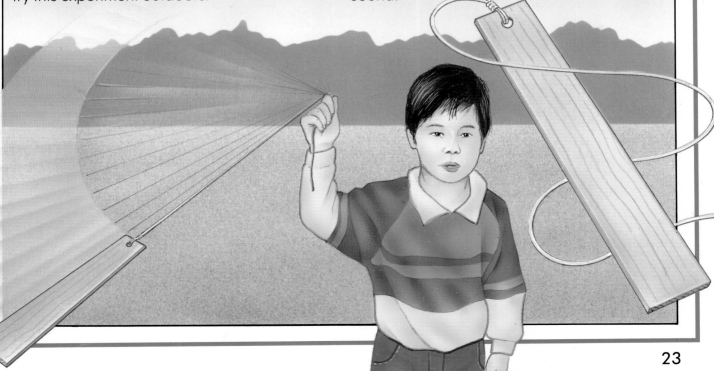

High and Low Notes

When musicians talk about the **pitch** of a note, they mean that one note sounds higher or lower than another. There are many different ways of changing the pitch of a note and you will be able to investigate some of them by trying these experiments.

▶ An orchestral xylophone. Each length of wood produces a different note when hit; the longer the wood, the deeper the note.

Underwater Recorder

For this experiment, you will need an old, plastic recorder and a tall jug full of water.

Cover all the holes on the recorder with your fingers. (If you find this difficult, stick some tape over the holes.) Blow gently into the recorder and you should hear a single, low-pitched note.

Take a deep breath and blow into the recorder while you push it into the jug of water. What happens to the pitch of the note? Take another breath and blow into the recorder again while you pull it up out of the water. How does the sound change?

How it works
When you blow into the recorder, the air inside it vibrates and you hear a note. The pitch of the note depends on the length of the column of air inside the recorder. When you push the recorder under the water, the water fills up the tube so the column is shorter. You hear a high-pitched note. As you pull the recorder out of the water, the column of air becomes longer and the note sounds lower.

Make a Glass Xylophone

Find four glass beakers which are about the same size and shape. Fill one beaker with water almost to the top. In the second beaker, make the water level come about 2 cm (0.8 inches) from the top of the glass. In the third beaker, make the level 4 cm (1.6 inches) from the top. Don't put any water in the fourth glass.

How to play your xylophone
Tap the side of each glass very gently with a wooden spoon. Each glass will ring with a note of a different pitch. Which glass makes the highest sound and which one makes the lowest sound?

How it works
When you tap each glass, it makes the water in the glass vibrate. The pitch of the note depends on the amount of water in the glass. With more water, the pitch of the note is lower.

More things to try
Try experimenting with different glasses and different amounts of water and see if you can play a tune on your glass xylophone.

Singing Wine Glass

Another way to make music with glass is to rub the edge of a wine glass.

You will need about 2 cm (0.8 inches) of water in the bottom of a wine glass. Hold the base of the glass firmly on the table top with one hand. Wet a finger of the other hand in the water, and rub the wet finger slowly and gently round the rim of the glass.

Experiment by rubbing harder and softer until you find that you can make the glass 'sing' with a clear note. It takes a little practice to get this to work.

More things to try
Try the same experiment with different amounts of water in the glass. How does the pitch of the note change?

Packing Case Bass

Equipment: A packing case or large, wooden crate, a broom handle, some string, a nail, a hammer.

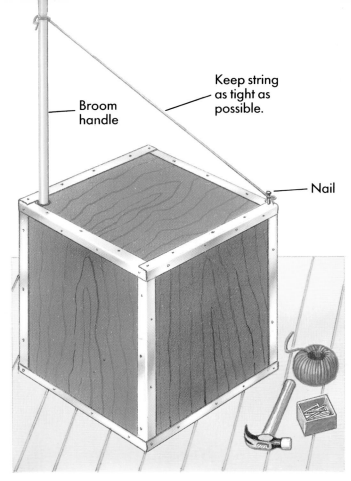

Broom handle

Keep string as tight as possible.

Nail

1. Ask an adult to help you make a hole in one corner of the bottom of the packing case or crate.
2. Fit the broom handle through the hole.
3. Tie one end of the string tightly to the top of the broom handle.
4. Use the hammer to tap a nail into the lid of the case or crate on the opposite side to the broom handle.
5. Tie the other end of the string round the nail so the string is stretched tight.

How it works

You will produce a rich, deep note because the crate acts like a very large sound box and amplifies the note. If you pull the broom handle back to tighten the string, the pitch of the note will get higher. If you allow the string to become looser, the note will get lower. With practice, you should be able to play simple tunes on your packing case bass.

How to play your bass

Put your foot on the case or crate to hold it steady. Hold the broom handle in one hand and use your other hand to twang the string.

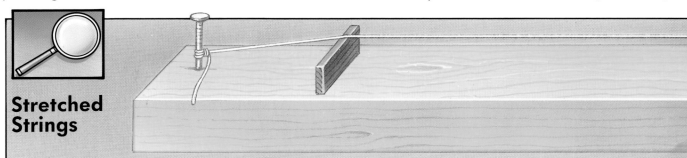

Stretched Strings

This investigation will help you to discover what happens to the sound made by a string when it is stretched.

Equipment: A length of nylon fishing line, a piece of wood about 3 cm (1 inch) thick and 60–90 cm (2–3 feet) long, a nail, a hammer, a small bucket, weights (such as small stones), two small pieces of wood about the size and shape of a thick ice-lolly stick.

1. Bang the nail firmly into one end of the wood.

2. Tie one end of the fishing line to the nail.
3. Place the wood on a table or work surface and pull the fishing line over the wood so it hangs over the side of the table.
4. Tie the bucket to the end of the fishing line.
5. Try to flick the line that is stretched along the wood. You will hear very little because it is rubbing against the wood and cannot vibrate freely.
6. To hold the fishing line above the wood, put a small piece of wood on its side at each end of the line.

Elastic Band Guitar

You can discover more about the effect of tight or slack strings by making this simple instrument.

Equipment: Several elastic bands of various lengths and thicknesses, a cardboard box (such as a shoe-box or a tissue box), scissors, 2 pieces of wood about 1 cm (0.4 inches) square and as wide as the box.

If you have a tissue box, it will probably already have a hole in the top. If you have an ordinary box, use the scissors to cut a hole in the top of the box.

Stretch the elastic bands across the top of the box leaving a gap of about 1 cm (0.4 inches) between each one. If you try to twang the bands, you will find that the sound is rather dull. The vibrations of the bands are muffled because they are rubbing against the top of the box.

If you look closely at a stringed instrument, such as a guitar, you will notice that the strings do not touch the body of the instrument. They are held above it by a piece of wood called the **bridge**.

Use the two pieces of wood to make a bridge for your guitar. When you twang the bands now, the sound will be much clearer. Is the pitch of the notes made by the looser bands higher

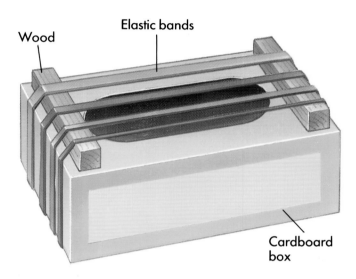

Wood

Elastic bands

Cardboard box

or lower than the notes made by the tightly-stretched bands? Experiment until you can play simple tunes on your elastic band guitar.

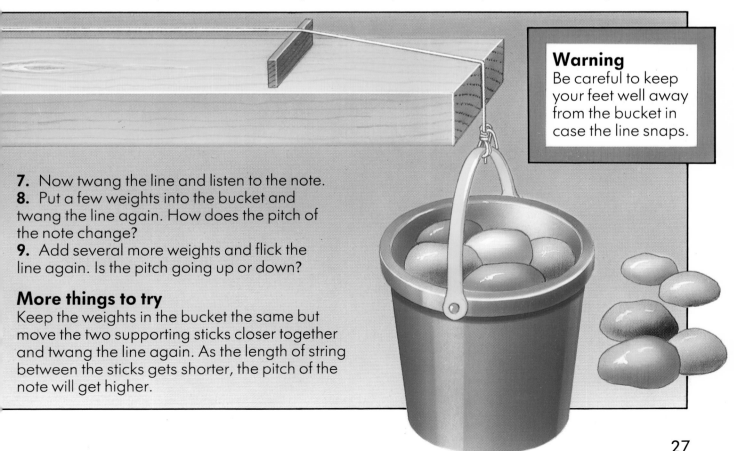

Warning
Be careful to keep your feet well away from the bucket in case the line snaps.

7. Now twang the line and listen to the note.
8. Put a few weights into the bucket and twang the line again. How does the pitch of the note change?
9. Add several more weights and flick the line again. Is the pitch going up or down?

More things to try
Keep the weights in the bucket the same but move the two supporting sticks closer together and twang the line again. As the length of string between the sticks gets shorter, the pitch of the note will get higher.

Music from Pipes

Instruments which musicians blow into to make musical sounds are made from wooden or metal pipes. The pipes produce a sound when the air inside them is made to vibrate. If the instrument is made from one very long piece of pipe, the pipe may be curled round in a circle or loop.

Instruments such as clarinets or oboes, in which the pipes are made from wood, are called **woodwind instruments**. Brass metal pipes are often used to make trumpets or trombones. These are called **brass instruments**.

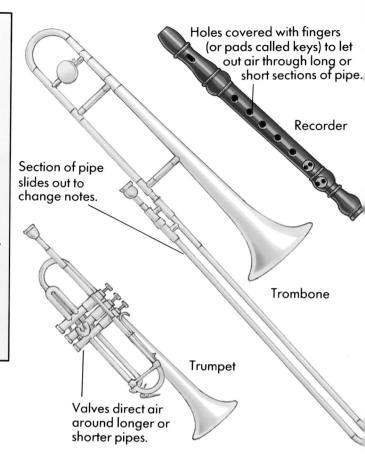

Holes covered with fingers (or pads called keys) to let out air through long or short sections of pipe.

Recorder

Section of pipe slides out to change notes.

Trombone

Valves direct air around longer or shorter pipes.

Trumpet

Bottle Music

All you need are five bottles of the same size and shape and some water.

Fill one bottle with water almost to the top. Fill the second bottle about three-quarters full, the third half full, the fourth a quarter full and leave the last bottle empty. To make the levels easier to see, you could colour the water with a few drops of ink or food colouring. Now try blowing across the top of each bottle.

How it works
When you blow across the top of each bottle, it makes the air inside the bottle vibrate. Small air spaces vibrate more rapidly than large air spaces. When there is very little air in the bottle, you produce a high note. When there is more air, the note is lower.

More things to try
Try the same experiment with different-sized bottles and different levels of water. How many notes can you make?

Blow across top of bottle.

Pipes of Pan

An instrument called Pan's pipes has been used for thousands of years in many different parts of the world.

Equipment: Several pieces of bamboo or hollow plastic piping, modelling clay, sticky tape, scissors.

1. Ask an adult to help you cut the pipes into different lengths so you have a range of lengths between 5 and 20 cm (2 and 8 inches).

2. Push a piece of modelling clay into the end of each tube or seal the end with sticky tape.

3. Arrange the pipes in order of length with the shortest pipe at one end and the longest pipe at the other end. Tape the pipes together so the open ends are exactly level with each other.

4. To play your Pan's pipes, place the edge of the open end of the pipe against your lower lip and blow gently across the top of the pipe.

5. What do you notice about the pitch of the notes from the different pipes?

▲ Chipaya Indians in Bolivia, South America, playing Pan pipes called *zamponas*.

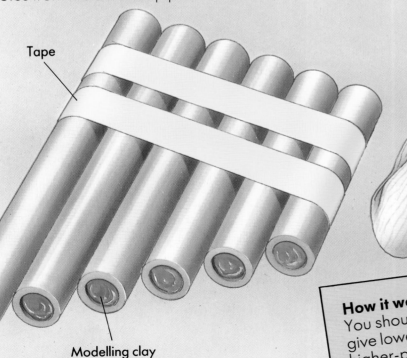

Tape

Modelling clay

How it works
You should discover that the longer pipes give lower notes and the shorter pipes make higher-pitched notes. With a little practice, you will be able to play tunes.

Reeds and Raspberries

Some woodwind instruments use **reeds** to make their musical sounds. When air is blown into the mouthpiece of these instruments, it makes the reeds vibrate, which in turn makes the air inside the pipe vibrate.

Brass instruments do not have reeds in the mouthpiece. Instead the musicians 'blow raspberries' to make their lips vibrate like reeds.

Make a Grass Squawker

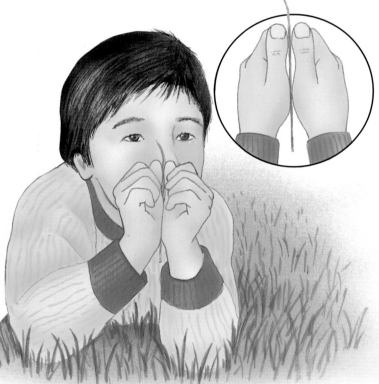

You can make a simple reed from a blade of grass. Choose a large blade of grass and hold it tightly between your thumbs and the heels of your hands.

Now blow hard between your thumbs over the edge of the grass blade. The grass will vibrate with a loud, squawking sound.

Make a Straw Reed

Another form of reed can be made from an ordinary drinking straw. Flatten the end of the straw and cut off the corners to match the diagram below.

Hold the cut end lightly between your lips and blow gently. As you blow, you force air between the straw 'reed' and make it vibrate. The vibrations of the reed make all the air in the straw vibrate in a certain way.

Flatten end of straw

Cut off ends like this.

More things to try
- Snip off half the straw. Does this make the sound higher or lower?
- In the middle of the straw, make a small cut like this.

Bend the straw up and down to vary the length of the column of air and change the notes.

Playing a Pipe

To see how brass instruments are played, find a piece of old piping about 1 metre (3 feet) long. Purse your lips to make a 'raspberry' sound and blow steadily down the pipe. To make different notes, press your lips more or less tightly together. This is how a bugle player plays simple bugle calls without using keys or valves to change the length of the column of air in the tube.

► Brass instruments are played in a different way from woodwind instruments. This trumpet player has to hold his lips tightly against the mouthpiece and 'blow a raspberry'. This makes his lips vibrate like a pair of reeds and sets off vibrations of the air inside the trumpet, which then produces musical sounds.

Shake, Rattle and Roll

For thousands of years, musicians throughout the world have made rhythm instruments, such as drums, shakers, blocks, bells and gongs. Anything that makes an interesting sound when it is hit or shaken can be used as an instrument. Instruments which are played like this are called **percussion instruments**. Many of these instruments can produce notes of only one pitch.

What is in the Box?

This game will test your friends' powers of hearing and detective work.

Equipment: Several small boxes or pots with tightly-fitting lids and a collection of small objects, such as paper clips, small pebbles, buttons, cotton-wool, marbles, polystyrene beads, dried peas, rice and drawing pins.

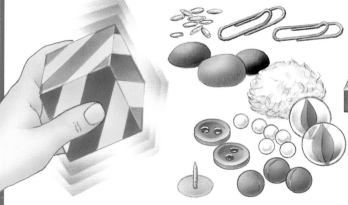

Put each kind of object into a different box and fit on the lid. Ask a friend to shake each box in turn. Then tell your friend that they are allowed to ask up to five questions about the contents of each box. You can only answer "Yes" or "No" to each question. See if your friend can guess what is inside each box.

Make a Shaker

Any empty plastic bottle can be used to make a shaker. You will also need a handful of objects such as small stones, dried peas, uncooked rice, conkers, buttons and small nuts and bolts.

Pour a small amount of one of the objects into the bottle and shake the bottle or twist it against the palm of your hand. Then try each of the other objects in turn to see which makes the best sound.
  When you have made a shaker with a sound that you like, tape the top firmly in place and paint the outside of the bottle .

Make a Drum

Equipment: Empty containers such as plastic bowls, cardboard boxes or tubes, plastic carrier bags, strong string, sticky tape, scissors, thin sticks or dowel.

1. Cut down the sides of the carrier bag and open it out to make one large sheet.

2. Place one of your containers on the plastic and cut around it allowing an extra 7–10 cm (3–4 inches) all round.

3. Ask a friend to help you pull the plastic tightly over the top of the container.

4. While your friend keeps the plastic skin stretched tight, tie string around the edge or use tape to keep the plastic in place.

5. To play your drum, tap it with your fingers or hit it gently with the thin sticks or dowel.

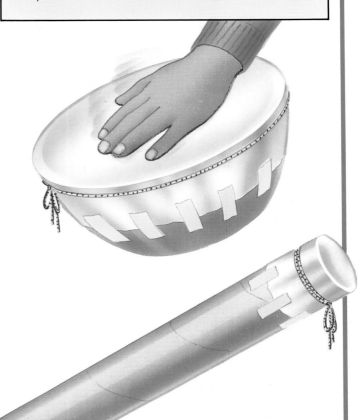

More things to try

● Try making drums of different sizes. To make a big bass drum, stretch a plastic bag over a large waste-paper bin. To make a tiny drum, use a small cardboard tube.

● Make the drum skins out of different materials, such a stiff paper, thin card or the rubber from a balloon.

Hint
To make a good sound, the plastic skin must be stretched as tightly as possible, without any wrinkles.

◀ Drummers in Kenya. Drums have been important instruments for thousands of years. They come in all shapes and sizes and can be made from a variety of materials from wood to plastic.

Tubular Bells

1. Ask an adult to help you cut the copper piping into 7 pieces. Make the smallest piece 5 cm (2 inches) long and then increase the length by 2.5 cm (1 inch) each time until you reach 20 cm (8 inches).
2. Tie the string or thread tightly round the end of each length of pipe.
3. Hang the pipes from a piece of wood resting across two chairs. Make sure the pipes hang clear of the ground.

Equipment: Many hardware shops sell lengths of copper piping for plumbing. Ask if they have any odd lengths left over or buy a piece about 1 metre (3 feet) long. You will also need thin string or strong thread, scissors, a piece of wood, two chairs, a large nail.

4. To play your pipes, tap them with the nail and listen to the ringing sound that they make. Which pipe makes the lowest note and which makes the highest note?

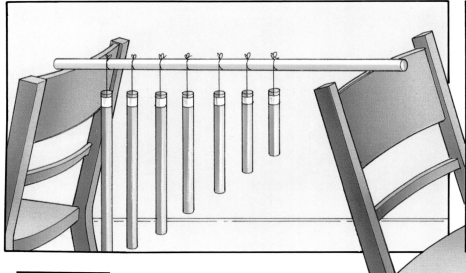

More things to try
Use nails to make a set of chiming bars. Find a nail of every length from about 5 cm (2 inches) to 20 cm (8 inches). Hang up the nails in the same way as the copper piping. Use a nail to play your nail chimes. The longer nails should produce a lower note than the shorter ones.

Playing the Spoons

You can make a very simple rhythm instrument from just two large spoons.

Hold both spoons in one hand with the handle of one spoon between your first and second finger and the handle of the other spoon between your thumb and first finger. Hold the spoons loosely with the bowl of each spoon touching.
   When you tap the lower spoon against the palm of your hand, the spoons will hit each other and make a clacking sound. Expert spoon players can tap spoons all over their bodies in time to music. Try this yourself.

Make a Whip Cracker

All you need are two old rulers, some paper, sticky tape and scissors.

Make a pad of paper about 3 cm (1 inch) long and place it between the two rulers at one end. Tape the rulers together around the paper pad. This will hold the rulers slightly apart; there should be a gap of about 0.5 cm (0.2 inches) between them.

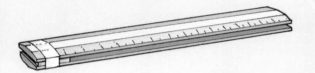

To play your whip cracker, hold it by the taped end and hit it against the palm of your hand. It makes a loud crack like a small whip and can be used as another percussion instrument, rather like castanets.

Make a Scraper

All you need are two wooden blocks, sandpaper, scissors, glue, drawing pins.

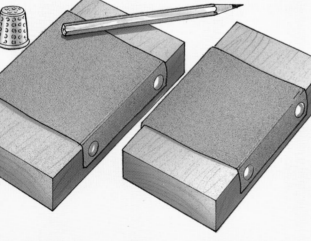

Cut two pieces of sandpaper to fit one side of each wooden block. Glue and pin the sandpaper firmly to the blocks. Hold one block in each hand and rub the sandpaper sides together.
    To make other scraping sounds, try rubbing a pencil over one of the pieces of sandpaper. Or put a thimble on one finger and scrape it over the sandpaper.

Balloon Sounds

Blow up a balloon and hold the neck of the balloon between the first fingers and thumbs of both hands. Pull the neck of the balloon into a narrow slit and let the air out slowly.

As the air escapes, it makes the rubber neck of the balloon vibrate, which produces a 'raspberry' noise. Tighten or loosen your hold on the neck of the balloon and see how many different sounds you can make.

Sound and Music

If you make several of the different instruments in the second half of this book, you can form a band with your friends. Make a stringed instrument, a woodwind instrument and percussion instruments. See if you can make up your own music. You could try setting a story to music or make up the sound effects for a play. When you have practised your music, ask an adult to help you record it.

Make a One-string Banjo

Here is another instrument for your band.

1. Use a sharp craft knife to cut two square holes at the front and back of the box just below the lid. The holes need to be big enough for the piece of wood to go through. (Ask an adult to help you with this.)

2. Push the long piece of wood through both holes so about 5 cm (2 inches) of the wood sticks out of the bottom hole. Glue or tape the wood firmly in place.

3. Screw one eyelet into the top end of the finger board and screw the other eyelet into the bottom end. Tie the fishing line or guitar string tightly between the two eyelets.

4. Use the two small pieces of wood to hold the string above the finger board. Put one piece beside the top eyelet screw and the other across the centre of the ice-cream box.

5. Tighten the string by screwing up the eyelets to take up the slack.

6. Paint your banjo in bright colours.

7. To play your banjo, hold the string tightly against the finger board and strum it gently. To make notes of a different pitch, hold down the string at different points along its length.

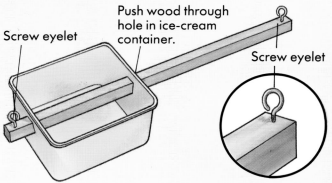

Screw eyelet

Push wood through hole in ice-cream container.

Screw eyelet

Screw eyelet

Equipment:
- A piece of wood about 90 cm (3 feet) long and 2–3 cm (about 1 inch) square.
- A large, empty ice-cream container with its lid taped firmly in place.
- A piece of fishing line or nylon or wire guitar string about 1 metre (3 feet) long. You will also need two screw eyelets, one for either end of the string.
- Two small pieces of wood to hold the string above the finger board.

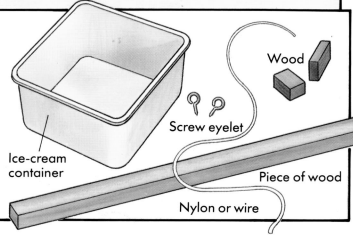

Wood

Ice-cream container

Screw eyelet

Piece of wood

Nylon or wire

Yogurt Pot Record Player

This experiment shows you how sounds are made by records.

You will need an empty yogurt pot and a pin. Use a thimble over the end of your finger or a pair of pliers to push the pin through the middle of the bottom of the pot.

Place the record on the record deck and switch it on. Hold the pot over the record so that the pin rests lightly in the grooves. When you put your ear to the pot, what can you hear?

How it works
The groove in a record is a spiral channel cut in the plastic. At the sides of the channel are tiny lumps and bumps (*see photograph below, right*). When the tip of the needle hits the bumps, it vibrates. The pot acts like a sound box and amplifies the vibrations.

Warning
You must use an old record and ask an adult to help you operate the record deck.

▲ The lumps and bumps in the groove of a record make the needle shake in different patterns of vibrations which we hear as music. This much-enlarged photograph shows a diamond stylus with the grooves of a record behind it.

◄ On an old gramophone like this, the needle fits into the end of a large horn, which (like the yogurt pot) makes the tiny vibrations in the tip of the needle loud enough for people to hear.

Animal Sounds

Animals such as birds, insects, fishes and mammals use sound signals for a variety of purposes, such as to warn others of danger or to attract a mate. The sounds they make carry messages such as "I live here, keep away," or "Look out, there's an enemy coming".

Most animals have ears to receive the sounds, although sometimes these are hidden from view. Birds have no outer ear flaps; their slit-like ears are hidden under their feathers. Fish have no outer or middle ear; they hear with part of the inner ear, which reacts to vibrations in the water. Insects have 'ears' in all sorts of unlikely places, such as on their legs or on the side of the abdomen.

Recording Animal Sounds

Try recording animal sounds such as birds singing, bees buzzing around flowers or animals at the zoo. An ordinary radio-cassette recorder works well. If possible, it is a good idea to use a recorder with a manual control for the recording level. A separate microphone is also useful. If you tape the microphone to a stick, it will not pick up sounds made by your fingers.

Before you start to record, make a note of the date, the place and the weather.

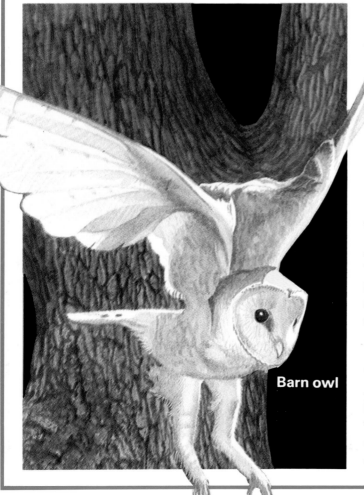

Barn owl

Warning Sounds

A grey squirrel makes a single, sharp snort or a "chuck-chuck charee" call to warn other squirrels of danger. If the squirrel decides to run away, it waves its tail over its back as it runs as a further warning to its neighbours.

Owl Radar Dish

A barn owl has very sensitive hearing which helps it to hunt for small animals at night. The white disc of feathers on a barn owl's face is an efficient sound collector which works rather like a radar dish.

Singing Whales

We do not know why whales sing, but we know that each whale has a different song. A typical song lasts for about ten minutes and a whale may repeat its song over and over again for 24 hours. Whales may sing to keep in touch with other whales. Sound travels well through water so whale songs, especially the low notes, may travel for hundreds of miles through the oceans.

Did you know that male mosquitoes are attracted to female mosquitoes by the sound of the females' wingbeats?

Thermometer Cricket

Temperature affects the rate of chirping in grasshoppers and crickets. The Snowy tree cricket has been called the 'thermometer cricket' because it is possible to calculate the temperature in Fahrenheit (very roughly) by adding 40 to the number of chirps it makes in 15 seconds.

▲ A few insects, such as this long-horned grasshopper, have well-developed hearing organs. On both the front legs, just below the 'knee', there are two slit-like openings through which sound enters the 'ears'. The 'ears' contain air sacs which act like sound boxes. Sensory cells on the air sacs respond to vibrations in the air.

▲ In the breeding season, Bullfrogs make loud sounds to attract females and drive other males away. The sounds are made by air being passed to and fro from the mouth to the lungs across the vocal cords. Some of the air enters air sacs in the floor of the mouth which inflate like a balloon and act as a sound box to make the sound louder.

Index

Editor: Nicola Barber
Designer: Ben White
Illustrators: Kuo Kang Chen
Peter Bull
Consultant: Barbara Taylor

Cover Design: Pinpoint Design
Picture Research: Elaine Willis

Photographic Acknowledgements
The publishers would like to thank the following for kindly supplying photographs for this book:
Page 4 Courtesy of Ray Alan; 5 Picturepoint; 10 Science Photo Library; 12 ZEFA; 14 Richard Bryant; 15 S. Dalton/NHPA; 16 ZEFA; 17 ARDEA; 20 NASA; 24 Clive Barda; 29 South American Pictures; 31 ZEFA; 33 ZEFA; 37 Paul Brierley (right), Edison National Historical Site (left); 39 S. Kraremann/NHPA (right), A. Bannister/NHPA (left)

KINGFISHER
Kingfisher Publications Plc
New Penderel House
283–288 High Holborn
London WC1V 7HZ

This reformatted edition published by
Kingfisher Publications Plc 1999
10 9 8 7 6 5 4 3 2 1
1TR / 0599 / SC / FR(FR) / 128MA
Originally published by Kingfisher Publications Plc 1989
© Kingfisher Publications Plc 1989

A CIP catalogue record for this book is available from the British Library.

ISBN 0 7534 0431 1

Printed in Hong Kong / China